LITTLE BLUE PENGUINS

LITTLE BLUE PENGUINS

Tales for Making the
Transition to Leadership

Strengths can become weaknesses and turn on you when you
least expect it.
—Dr. Richard Z. Gooding

TED BAUMHAUER Ed.D.

Copyright © 2008 by Ted Baumhauer Ed.D.

Library of Congress Control Number: 2008902930
ISBN: Hardcover   978-1-4363-3304-7
                Softcover   978-1-4363-3303-0

This book was printed in the United States of America.

To order additional copies of this book, contact:
Xlibris Corporation
1-888-795-4274
www.Xlibris.com
Orders@Xlibris.com
47609

CONTENTS

To the people who have taught me how to live:

My wife and children,
My parents and brothers,
and
My teachers at McDonald High School,
Thiel College, Springfield College and The University of Vermont.

ACKNOWLEDGMENTS

So many people in my life made this project possible. First of all, I have to thank my wife Jup and my three girls Molly, Emma, and Allie for their support and love over the years.

I also want to thank my friends; some of their great stories are in this book. Special thanks goes to Tom Murphy, Joe Broadus, Deb Nawoczenski and Paul Kempner. We have worked and learned together, and I appreciate their friendship greatly.

Along the way, I have been privileged to learn from some great teachers like Dr. Ken Fishell; Dr. Ken Hood; and Dr. Tom Patterson at The University of Vermont. At Springfield College, the direction of my whole career in leadership consulting came from Dr. Al Petitpas, whom I cannot thank enough. Also, you will read a story in this book about another great teacher at Springfield, Dr. Len Bosari.

Without these friends, my life would be far less than it is today and I thank every one of them!

Ted B.

Whatever you can do, or dream you can, begin it.
Boldness has genius, power, and magic in it.
—Goethe

The Little Blue Penguin symbol is intended to remind us that individuals can learn to take risks or to avoid them due to their environment. How we, and those around us, take on or avoid risk is a leadership issue. If our organizations are to survive and thrive, then it is vital that we take risks. Leaders then are responsible for creating an environment where risk is not just tolerated but taught, expected, and rewarded.

INTRODUCTION

I f you're reading this book, I'm assuming you either are a leader or are interested in becoming a leader. This book consists of stories that have helped me explain leadership concepts over the years. Some of the stories come from friends while others I've experienced firsthand. A few of the stories have been around for a while and are not original. I've included them because I believe they have an important leadership lesson to teach. All of these stories and experiences have helped me understand and teach many facets of leadership. Learning anything, especially something as complex as leadership, is an ongoing process. It is process that I am still engaged in on a daily basis.

At the end of each story, there will be the Questions to Ponder and Actions to Take. Use the questions and actions to take to assess how you and your organization are doing with the issues illustrated by the story. Write your answers and comments in the book and date them. Revisit the stories a couple of times a year to compare your answers and to see if anything has changed and to hopefully gauge your progress.

Please enjoy the book and the stories as you work to become a better leader.

Ted Baumhauer, EdD
Fairport, New York

There has been a lot of talk about leadership accountability
and the lack of it in a world today. Accountability isn't about
talk it is about action and taking control of your own life.
—Ted B.

Only I can change my life. No one can do it for me.
—Carol Burnett

A NOTE TO READERS: WHY STORY

D on't let the fact that I'm framing leadership in stories be confused that I think leading is easy. It's not. The reason I'm using the stories is that facts and theories disappear over time. We don't remember them. When I get into a tough situation, a two-by-two window doesn't pop into my head. In most situations, my brain is looking for something I can relate to, some example, that will help me resolve the situation, in other words, a familiar story.

So being a leader is hard, and if you're going to be a good one, you'll make mistakes and maybe get hurt.

Confucius said, "If you make a mistake and do not correct it, this is called a mistake" (15:30, from *The Essential Confucius* by Thomas Cleary).

GET IN THE GAME!

A good friend of mine, Carl, told me this story when he was playing freshman (HS) football. His grandfather lived with them at the time and he was on the sidelines watching the game. Carl was excited to be playing his first game and proud that his grandfather was there to see it.

Carl's grandfather was a Scotsman. Not just any Scotsman, though. He was a decorated member of Scotland's famed Black Watch Regiment in World War I.

During the middle of the game, Carl got roughed up. He noticed that he was bleeding and took himself out of the game. As he came off the field with a huge raspberry on his leg, he found a spot on the bench.

Sitting there looking at his leg bleeding, he noticed that his grandfather was standing beside him. Slowly his grandfather leaned over and with his thick Scottish accent, whispered, "Lad, it's a good two feet from your heart. You're a long way from dead. Get back in the game!"

Get in and stay in. Our biggest victories aren't the ones that come easily; they are the ones that we struggled to achieve. They are the ones that the outcome was in doubt until the very end. Get in the game and stay in even if you get hurt!

Questions to Ponder

What opportunity are you holding yourself back from?

Why?

Did you already make an attempt, but got hurt?

What did you gain/learn from that experience?

What did you lose?

What in your current situation would be better if you hadn't taken that chance?

Would you take that chance again?

What opportunity is your department or group avoiding?

What is holding you back?

The only people who never fail are those who never try.

—Ilka Chase

Effort is only effort when it begins to hurt.

—José Ortega y Gassel

NAVIGATING THE MAZE

W hile I was living in Vermont, I discovered the power of experiential learning from a gentleman named Paul Kempner at Rock Point School. Experiential learning involves exercises that challenge individuals and groups to use their communication, problem solving, or leadership skills. These activities have become a staple of my training sessions.

Paul was an excellent teacher, and he taught me the power of these "games." When I moved to Rochester, New York, I wanted to connect with people like Paul who were teaching on and with ropes courses. That search led me to Linda Fox and her program at Keuka College. The day I observed, she ran the group through several of the exercises I was familiar with and a couple that I hadn't seen before. The exercise that made the biggest impression on me that day was the maze.

The maze is just that, a maze of strings set up in a stand of trees. Participants are led to the maze while they are blindfolded, so they never see the maze until they have completed the task. When they arrive at the maze, the participants are led, one at a time, to random places inside the maze while they are still blindfolded. Once all the participants are inside the maze, the instructors place themselves just outside the strings on the perimeter.

The group is then told of their situation and that they need to find their way out by following the strings and that they are not to duck under them. When the first couple of participants work their way out, they are given a choice: they can take their blindfold off and stay out or keep their blindfold on and reenter the maze to lead others out.

From what the staff at Keuka College told me, that is how all groups go through the maze activity with one exception. The exception is the group from AA (Alcoholics Anonymous) on their first trip to Keuka's ropes course. The only difference is when the instructors are finished placing all the participants inside the web, they quietly tie off the only exit with a string that they kept hidden in their pocket. With no way out, the blindfolded participants are left inside the maze, searching for an exit that isn't there until they ask for help.

However long it takes to ask for help is how long they stay in the maze. The lesson is that the participants in this group are in a situation that they cannot get out of on their own just like being an alcoholic. They may not want help and/or think they can do it on their own, but they can't and they need to admit that as a fact.

Learning how to be an effective leader can be a huge undertaking. You may need to ask for help along the way from any number of people. Asking for help is not necessarily a sign of weakness. It can be a sign of strength when working harder and longer isn't going to help. In this case, you're saying I need to work smarter but I don't know what that means yet and seek out someone or ones who can guide you. Asking for help can be the most courageous and smartest thing you can do to get better as fast as possible.

Questions to Ponder

What roadblock(s) have you run into as a leader?

Who have you talked to about this?

Who else can you talk to about this?

What can you do to deepen your knowledge based on this type of problem?

The road to success is always under construction.
—Arnold Palmer

Being defeated is often a temporary condition. Giving up is what makes it permanent.
—Marilyn vos Savant

Section 1

Base Content Capacity

Why Do Groups Fail?

B efore we get started, I have a question to ask you. What are some reasons that groups fail?

What is your experience?

What behaviors did they do or didn't do that you believe led to their failure?

List them here.

We'll get back to these reasons later.

A COMMON STORY

P eter Principal gets hired by a company to do a job. Pete gets very little guidance or coaching as to how to do a good job. However, Pete is smart, bright, and doggone it, people like him! He is a self-starter and commits to being not only good but also great. He puts in long hours and keeps his nose to the grindstone. Over time, Pete thrives and becomes a shining star in this job. About that time, Pete notices that something else is happening: his supervisor gets the credit for developing his talent as a young rising star. The reality is that the supervisor had very little to do with Pete becoming a success; it was his own commitment, hard work, and long hours. But maybe that was the plan: hire potentially good employees and stay out of their way. After a time, we can assess their performance on the job, keeping the good and productive employees and getting rid of the rest.

To me this all seems like a numbers game.

"Luck is probability taken personally." Chip Denman

Just because benign neglect produces a productive employee, on occasion, does not validated that style of leadership. Here's the case against this style. What happens to all the other, potentially good, employees who don't get past the lack of training and guidance? The ones who don't invest their time and energy to figure it out? Do you fire them? Well, you could, but who is accountable for all that time and productivity lost while they were struggling? What about the productivity that's lost after you fire them until you can fill the position again? Who covers for that and who is responsible? In both cases, it is their supervisor.

Now what if that same supervisor, or someone trained to coach, worked closely with all new hires or anyone taking on a new responsibility to bring them up to speed? That would be costly until the employees got a handle on their new responsibilities. Think of that time and effort to coach as an investment. Some investments pay out and some don't. The employees still might not grow into their new responsibilities and become productive. Yes, that is true. In that case, we would have spent extra time and effort with them that didn't pay off.

There is still a benefit of staying close to them during the first stages while they are learning to do their job. If they didn't get it and were not going to become productive employees, we would know much sooner and not lose a lot of time and money while they were not producing. By staying close to those with new tasks and responsibilities, we can teach them to do it the way we want it done from the very beginning and continually determine their level of competence. Once they have proven they can produce, we can cut them loose to do their jobs independently. If they don't show signs of being able to work independently, we will know it sooner and be able to take the appropriate action to ensure ongoing productivity. That's what a leader is supposed to do.

Questions to Ponder

Who in your work group has been taking on new responsibilities?

How much extra time and attention are they getting to teach them how to handle and successfully take on these new skills?

How closely is their work checked with the goal of building both their skill and confidence so that they can eventually work independently with confidence?

My main job was developing talent. I was a gardener providing water and other nourishment to our top 750 people. Of course, I had to pull out some weeds, too.

—Jack Welch

THE MODEL
ICEBERG CAREER

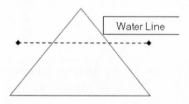

Water Line

Think of your career
as an iceberg.
Let's say this iceberg is in the
shape of a triangle. Above the
waterline are all your content skills
that you need to do your job.

These are skills that you have learned on the job or gone to school to learn. Examples of these skills include the following: how to program a computer, how to build a computer, how to research a legal case, how to diagnose and treat a patient, how to design a building, how to build a budget, and how to run a machine. You will be successful, personally, by how well you carry out these tasks. So your personal skill determines your success.

Eventually, you will be asked to be on a team with other employees or maybe even to lead a team of people who have the same, or similar, skills. At this point, your success is no longer based just on how well you do your task; it is, at least partially, based on how well you work with others to accomplish a goal. Even if you are the smartest and most skilled in the task, that won't matter much if the group doesn't listen to you and work with you toward the goal.

Working on a team, which is below the waterline on our iceberg career, you are dealing with a new set of skills: process skills. Even if you never become the leader of the group, you still need to combine your personal skills with team skills to be successful. If you are the leader, you not only need to hone your team skills but also your facilitation skills to bring out the best in each member of your team. Leaders need to facilitate planning and problem solving on a regular basis. This is clearly not the same skill set as those above the waterline. The game has changed!

This new set of skills is often called the soft skills while skills like accounting, budgeting, and finance are called the hard skills. In reality, they are both hard—one set is perceived as messier than the other, and we know which one.

Going below the waterline to develop this new skill set means paying attention to a different set of inputs. Leaders are interested in who contributes to their group. By default that also means they are interested in who doesn't contribute.

Leaders often strive to even out the playing field. If all your ideas come from the same person or the same couple of people, why are the rest included? On the other hand, if someone is on the team and they never contribute, that's also not okay! A leader addresses this and gets input and feedback from all the members of the team, not just a few. This may mean the leader has to comfort the afflicted and afflict the comfortable. If that has to happen to get or keep the group effective, the leader steps up and does the job.

The leader pays a great deal of attention to how decisions are made. Decisions that impact the success of the company are too important to leave to the few vocal enough to express their opinions. A leader's job, in good part, is to teach the group how to set goals and plan to achieve them together. At times, getting the team to focus on the goal and not letting them attack each other takes a tremendous amount of effort. At other times, though, it is easy. But most of the time it's hard.

If you doubt that last statement, listen to the conversation in the next meeting you go to. Where is the focus? Is it on addressing the goal/problem, or is it on attacking another person and their idea(s)? Is what's being said adding light to the situation, or does it add heat? Someone (the leader whether in name or function) has to step in and redirect the group to attack the problem. Left alone, most groups erode to individuals pushing for their solution and dismissing other potential solutions.

A leader puts their focus on behaviors that keep the group from being successful. Remember that list I asked you to make: Why do groups fail? Look at your answers. Where are your answers, above the waterline or below? When I have asked this question in my training classes, the answers run about 90 to 99 percent in the below-the-waterline category.

Groups don't usually fail because they don't know what to do. Even if they don't know the answer to a content problem, the group will go out and hire a content expert, like a computer programmer or lawyer or accountant. If the company bought a new piece of machinery and couldn't get it to run at the levels they were promised, they would go back to the firm they bought it from and bring in someone to teach them how to run it. Groups can and do fail because of content problems, but not as often as process issues. Look at your list again. It is probably full of process issues. Who can control those problems? The group can, but it is hard and messy; they need leadership to focus on them and address them. That's the work of the leader!

Where are you in terms of your success? Is it based on your personal skill or the skill of others who report to you?

How often does your work group talk about how to function better as a team? If you asked, "What's keeping us from being more successful?" all you would get is that they need more money, time, equipment, and so on. You will need another approach to get at this issue. Put the focus on the positive and ask them what do strong teams do and how they could incorporate those behaviors.

If you focus on process skills, even if you aren't the designated leader, your group can become much stronger. Someone needs to; otherwise, it will never happen.

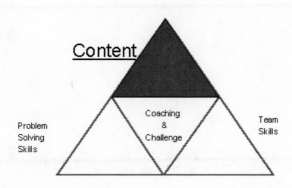

Content versus Process Skills

Content skills get you your first job. Content skills are the technical skills you need to do a job, like how to run a machine, prepare a legal brief, or make a sale. These are the skills that drive your personal success early in your career.

On their own, they are enough to build a career. They will only take you so far. Eventually you will be asked to be on a team and to work with other people and potentially even to lead a group. To be successful you will need to discover and develop your team skills. Without these skills you will likely be limited in how successful you might become because jobs that let you work alone, isolated, usually report to someone who isn't alone and isolated.

RUBBER LIPPING

W hile I was living in Vermont and working at UVM, I took several classes in American sign language. It is a great and expressive language. One of my favorite ASL signs is sometimes used by deaf people when referring to hearing people. It isn't very complimentary but it makes the point exactly. It is the sign for "gossip" or "rubber lipping."

What this term means in reference to hearing people is that we can and do, sometimes, say things we don't believe or intend to do. It is a reminder to not just "listen" to the words but also watch the actions.

The same thing can be said about leaders. When we are in the leadership role, people will constantly judge what we say and what we do. If the words are not consistent with our actions, we are "rubber lipping." Our reputation will develop based on that inconsistency. But if what we say and what we do match up, then we can be trusted to be true to our word.

Where are the words inconsistent with the actions in your department? Organization? Your own leadership? Ask for other people's perspectives on this.

Listen without reacting to whatever they tell you because what they tell you is a gift. It is a gift that, if you use it, can make your organization more consistent and stronger because it will be more worthy of trust (trustworthy).

Questions to Ponder

What is the sense of trust in your group/department?

What are people kept in the dark about?

What are the inconsistencies that you see between what people say and what they do?

How are those issues being addressed? If they are not being addressed, why not?

A certain pupil asked Confucius about government, "What are the four evils?"

Confucius replied,

"To execute without having admonished; this is called cruelty.

To examine accomplishments without having instructed; this is called brutality.

To be lax in direction yet make deadlines; this is called viciousness.

To be stingy in giving what is due to others; this is called being bureaucratic."

(20:4, from *The Essential Confucius* by Thomas Cleary page 37)

MAGICIANS AND JUGGLERS

U pon the occasion of the anniversary of my birth, one with a zero in it, my wife surprised me with a trip to Las Vegas. A highlight for me was seeing the Lance Burton Magic Show. This was a highlight primarily because I got to see Michael Goudeau perform and to talk with him after the show. As a juggler, I was a fan of his, and my wife went the extra steps to contact him to arrange the meeting.

If you haven't seen the show, it was a well-done production. Mr. Burton performed his magic for the first thirty or forty minutes and then introduced Michael as his special guest juggler. My first impression was that the audience would hate this. They paid to see a magic show and here comes a juggler? Sitting in the audience, I was ready to cringe. Michael took the stage and in sixty seconds, the audience loved him! They cheered for him as he finished his set and Mr. Burton retook the stage. Every time he appeared onstage in the second half of the show, the audience immediately reacted!

This got me thinking about the differences between performing magic and juggling. When you see a good juggler or magician, you know they have a great deal of skill and have spent hours of time practicing. There is a big difference, though, in how they go about entertaining an audience.

Magicians use a number of techniques to conceal their skills and abilities to amaze and amuse us. Jugglers on the other hand (that was a pun, wasn't it?) want us to see and appreciate their skills. If you have any doubts about this, here is an assignment. The next time you see a magic show, pick one trick they did; and after the show, ask them how they did it, what technique did they used, or some other question like that. I'll bet you won't get any useful information. Why should you? If a magician has spent any amount of money buying and learning the trick, it is not in their best interest to just give it away. The better or higher cost of the trick to buy or build, the less likely the magician will tell you.

A juggler has a different perspective. Just because you have the juggling props doesn't mean you can juggle and even if you know how to do a trick doesn't mean you can do it. In fact, if you did have the props and knew how hard the trick was, you might actually appreciate the juggler's skills even more. Now, the same could be said for the magician. Both juggling and magic require a great deal of skill to do well. The difference to me is how they display or hide their skills.

There are ways to find out how magicians do their magic. The art form has always had a sense of secrecy about it, though. For good reason, if you knew how the tricks were done, the "magic" would be gone. A lot of the power of the magician disappears. That's not to say you still wouldn't be amazed at the ingenuity, dexterity, and skill involved, but the surprise and therefore a lot of the magician's power to entertain is gone.

To learn how to juggle, you can do the same things: join a group and ask experts. There doesn't seem to be the same sense of secrecy, though, even if there are some secret techniques here and there. Who does what trick isn't limited by not sharing information; it's limited by the difficulty of the trick itself. It is pretty easy to find someone to tell you or show you on the Internet how to do almost any juggling trick.

Questions to Ponder

When you lead a group are you more like a magician or a juggler?

Why do you think that?

Where are decisions made, out in the open or behind closed doors? What information is shared with your group?

How much does your group know about how things really get done?

What affects everyone can best be solved by everyone.

—Anonymous

Arthur C. Clarke formulated the following three "laws" of prediction:

1. When a distinguished but elderly scientist states that something is possible, he is almost certainly right.
2. When he states that something is impossible, he is very probably wrong.
3. The only way of discovering the limits of the possible is to venture a little way past them into the impossible. Any sufficiently advanced technology is indistinguishable from magic.

EFFICIENT VERSUS EFFECTIVE

M any times these two words are used interchangeably. Who wouldn't like their organization to be more efficient? Yet they do have slightly different meanings. *Webster's New Collegiate Dictionary* defines the two words as follows: *effective*, "producing a decided, decisive, or desired effect," *efficient*, "being or involving the immediate agent in producing an effect." The difference is that being effective produces desired effects; it is doing the right thing(s). Being efficient means taking action to get immediate results. Being efficient gets immediate results, and being effective gets the right results. In order to be successful over the long haul we may need to slow down to be effective before we become efficient.

Doing what is right first is a better use of time than just doing something to get immediate results. This applies to the people you work with and especially training on the job. Steven Covey said, "You can be efficient with things but with people you have to be effective." Teaching someone how to do a task on the job is best done right the first time. How much time is wasted training the same person over and over again? In the book *The Leadership Engine*, Noel Tichy suggests that excellent companies are not only learning organizations but also teaching organizations. Excellent companies reward those that know how to teach and mentor. By cultivating the skill of teaching, these companies are grooming the next generation and are able to reinvent themselves in the next economy. Organizations that can develop a talent pool will be the long-term winners.

The difference between effective and efficient may be small but it can produce huge differences in an organization over the long haul.

Questions to Ponder

What systems or methods has your group/department assessed and updated in the last year?

What systems or methods in your department need to be updated?

What does your group/department do well? What are the critical measures of success for your group/department? How well do these two match up?

How might you be more effective in your organization?

People, like nails, lose their effectiveness when they lose direction and begin to bend.

—Walter Savage Landor

Section 2

Core Team Skills

Psychologists have observed that bad habits can spread through an office like a contagious disease. Employees tend to mirror the bad behaviors of their co-workers, with factors as diverse as low morale, poor working habits, and theft from the employer all rising based on the negative behavior of peers.

—Greene, 1999, *The 100 Simple Secrets of Successful People* by David Niven, PhD

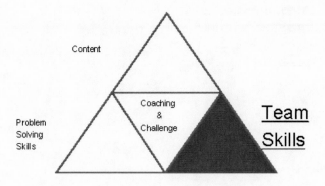

RIGHTEOUS INDIGNATION

O ver the last thirty years, a good friend of mine, Tom Murphy, has performed all over the world. His performance includes a fair amount of gymnastics and physical comedy. One of my favorite routines he does involves a unicycle and an audience volunteer.

The routine starts with Tom trying to mount the unicycle. Despite his best attempts he is unable to get on and stay on the thing. This leads him out into the audience in search of a volunteer to help him achieve his goal.

When the two of them return to the stage, the volunteer is asked to hold the unicycle in front of the audience with both hands. Tom explains that he is going to get behind her, run up, and launch himself over her shoulders onto the unicycle and ride off. Not a problem!

As he runs up to the volunteer and puts his hands on her shoulders, she naturally push up to take his weight. At this point, Tom ducks down, puts his head between her legs, lifts them up, and mounts the unicycle!

Over a thirty-year career, he has done this over a thousand times. One of his victims has included the reigning Miss America who was in a full evening gown. This is a stunt he has got down. Understandably, this stunt makes people in the audience a little uncomfortable and the laughter follows.

A few years ago, Tom was performing on a cruise ship. As is typical on cruises, there are two shows each night. The performers just repeat their acts in the late show.

Tom did his forty-minute set in the first show, had some dinner, and waited around for the second show. As he was standing in the wings to be introduced by the assistant cruise director, he got a surprise. The assistant told him that the volunteer-on-the-shoulders bit was too dangerous and that he couldn't do it as part of his set. At that point, the assistant walked on to the stage and introduced him!

Knowing that a full ten minutes of a forty-minute set had just been wiped out, Tom had a decision to make.

He could

1. not do the bit and cut his set short,
2. do it anyway,
3. substitute something in to try and cover the ten minutes that fit with the rest of his material, and
4. just not do the forty-minute set and walk away.

That's a lot to think about with no time to prepare. On top of that, you're mad about the situation and you're performing onstage. He chose to substitute something into the act to fill the forty minutes. But did I mention he was MAD! Who wouldn't be?

There was a good two hours between shows that he could have prepared something to cover those ten minutes. Why didn't the assistant cruise director tell him immediately after the first show?

From the assistant's perspective, he knew Tom would be mad and argue to keep the piece in the set. By telling him at the last minute, he was trying to avoid the argument he knew was going to happen.

And that is exactly what happened, Tom got mad! He got mad at the moment he was walking onstage to do a forty-minute set. Did the assistant want him to do a good show? My guess is, yes, he wanted Tom to do a good show. Did his last minute feedback account for that? Probably not, the focus was on avoiding a confrontation, not on preparing the performer to do a good show. The funny thing about this is that by waiting until the last minute to give feedback on the first show guaranteed Tom would react badly, fulfilling the assistant's worst fear. Sounds like a self-fulfilling prophecy!

If Tom had done anything but what he did, the assistant could have fired him. What a use of power! Set him up to behave badly and then hold it against him for doing exactly that! Forget about putting on a good performance and doing a good job, though.

On the other hand, walking out onstage, was Tom thinking about putting on a good show? Probably not! He was thinking about what to do, how to cover it, and what he was going to say to the assistant after getting off the stage.

Did they both want a great performance? Yes! Is that what they were thinking about and what their behaviors suggested? No! The most important thing, the performance, got lost and the focus was on confrontation. Avoiding confrontation and setting the other person up to want a confrontation became the focus.

> Assistant Cruise Director: See, I knew he would react badly! I don't want to deal with that!

> Murph: They didn't give me a chance! See, they don't treat their performers well!

Each mind-set leads to behavior that creates a self-fulfilling prophecy. Neither one wants to step back and put the focus on what they both want, which is a good show.

Questions to Ponder

> Where in your organization are people focused more on protecting themselves than the main thing?

What do different departments say and think about other departments?

Do they treat them in a way that validates what they already believe? By doing that, they keep the focus off the most important task, working together as one team! No organization needs that!

If you think the problem is out there, that thought is the problem.
—Stephen Covey

One cool judgment is worth a thousand counsels. The thing to do is to supply light and not heat.
—Woodrow Wilson

Sociology maxim: "If you believe something is real, it is real in its consequences."

HOW EASY IT IS TO ASSUME

T ry to read this. It is amazing!

Trhee is an ubarn mtyh taht our bairn is clabpae of rdeinag wodrs wtih jeulmbd leetrts as lnog as the fsirt and lsat lrttees are in the crecrot pcale. The mtyh cnetnods taht it is beasd on recrsaeh form Cigdbrmae Uvinirsety. Wlihe it is utnure taht tihs has been cifmneord wtih rsaeecrh at any utiisevrny our brians are albe to dcdeoe slracebmd wdros if tehy aern't too dclffuiit. So waht mghit tihs say aoubt our biarn's and teihr ablitiy to amssue and flil in the balnks to let us see waht we wnat to see?

Our brains are truly amazing. We constantly fill in the blanks of information and make decisions; we have to do this, otherwise we wouldn't be able to function. This ability can be a strength and lead to timely and insightful decisions. There is a downside, though. Strengths overused can become weaknesses, and the skill of filling in the blanks is certainly an example of that. Assuming we know the whole story without finding out what the rest of the team sees, and believes, can lead us to our worst disasters.

This is the story of the "Emperor's New Clothes." It's not a new story, but leaders still surround themselves with people who tell them only what they want to hear, people who don't or won't question their thinking. The original role of the court jester was to question the king and queen's thinking and to make fun of their decisions, big and small. The royalty that used jesters in this way were smart enough to know there were other perspectives on any issue and that, with the power of life and death, they would certainly be surrounded by "Yes Men!"

Today's leaders may not have the power of life and death, and yet unemployment doth make cowards of us all to paraphrase. Have we killed, or fired, all the jesters? Hopefully not!

Questions to Ponder

What are some of the assumptions in your group/department?

For example, what are the top four or five most important measures of success for your group/department?

Check with each member of the team in a group or individually and see if they list the same measures.

Do they? If not, there are some pretty big assumptions being made that need to be addressed now!

Everyone is pulling the group in different directions by doing what they think is right. Get them pulling in the same directions as soon as possible. They are trying to do the right thing, help them.

Translation

There is an urban myth that our brain is capable of reading words with jumbled letters as long as the first and last letters are in the correct place. The myth contends that it is based on research from Cambridge University. While it is untrue that this has been confirmed with research at any university our brains are able to decode scrambled words if they aren't too difficult. So what might this say about our brain's and their ability to assume and fill in the blanks to let us see what we want to see?

Do not let what you cannot do interfere with what you can do.
—John Wooden

WHY DO GROUPS FAIL?
PART 2

S o did you think of one or two reasons why groups fail? If you didn't,
write them down, do that now.

Why Do Groups Fail?

List those reasons here.

Look at your list: does it contain mostly content or process reasons? Are
there any content reasons on your list at all? If there are, there probably
aren't that many.

Why? In a word, attention.

Groups are more likely to pay attention to a failing to achieve as their
core reason for existing. If there is confusion about how an important piece
of machinery runs, they will clear up that by training or calling in an expert.
They won't fail because they didn't pay attention to that issue. Same with
computer, legal, marketing, etc., if it is some content issue, the problem
can be solved by attention, effort, training, money, or an expert.

Content skills are hard skills. They can be defined, and you can measure
them. Are we better, more productive, quicker, producing more today and
at a higher standard than yesterday?

The Peter principle is based on competent workers being promoted to a higher level where the skills of the new position are beyond their capacity to learn or perform. The promotion from content expert and team member to team leader is a transition that creates an environment for the Peter principle. They've risen to their level of incompetence if they cannot learn and display a new set of skills to lead others. And yet content leadership has its place.

Content leadership is effective and efficient. It works best in emergency situations. When there isn't time to develop other's skills and self-confidence, a decision has to be made now. That's the time to go with the person who has got the most experience, training, and knowledge. If that's your way of leading all the time, though at some point probably sooner than later, that could become a limitation in your career and the Peter principle kicks in.

Questions to Ponder

What do you believe to be good team behavior?

Make a list.

At your next opportunity, ask a coworker to make their list. Compare the two. Negotiate any differences.

Continue the process until your whole team has one list.

Does your group/department have a list of team ground rules?

How were they developed?

Did someone give them to you, or did the group create them? If the group created their own ground rules, that is more powerful.

Who, if anyone, in your group reminds them of the ground rules and holds them accountable to follow them?

Each of us is either a part of the problem or a part of the solution.

—Eldridge Cleaver

EVEN PIRATES HAD
RULES OF CONDUCT

When you think of a typical pirate, what comes to mind? I don't mean pirates from the movies but real pirates from the 1600 and 1700s. What were they like, what did they care about?

In 2005, I was driving around Rochester, New York, and I heard a radio interview on National Public Radio with a gentleman who had written a book on pirates. In the interview, he mentioned that there were differences between pirates, buccaneers, and privateers. The main difference was in their having permission from at least one government to steal from another.

Privateers worked under the flag of at least one country, buccaneers sometimes did, and pirates were self-employed. For the countries that used their services, it was an easy way to gain revenue; they, of course, got a share of the booty without having to officially fund a navy.

Back to the interview, the author mentioned that while the groups' motivations were slightly different they all did share a common code of behavior called the Brethren or Custom of the Coast. There were slight differences from ship to ship depending on the captain at the time, but there were a lot of common standards of behavior that they held each other to that surprised me. The Brethren of the Coast paints a different picture of the pirates and how they worked together than I first imagined.

Here are some of the rules that were typically part of their code. They surprised me and might surprise you too.

- They negotiated their version of the Code together and were clear about the consequences before they left port. Everyone had to sign on the dotted line to be a member of the crew. After they set sail anyone who wanted to join the crew had to sign on to their code.
- Every crewmember, from captain to cabin boy, had one vote in affairs of the moment. This held true except for times of crisis, like when they were attacking another ship or being chased. In those situations the captain had command.
- No striking another member of the crew while on board. All quarrels to be ended on shore at sword and pistol.
- No person to game at cards or dice for money.
- The captain and quarter-master to receive two shares of a prize; the master, boatswain, and gunner, one share and a half; and other officers, one and a quarter.
- Every man to be called fairly in turn, by list, on board of prizes. If they defrauded the Company to the value of a dollar, in plate, jewels, or money, marooning was their punishment.
- The lights and candles to be put out at eight o'clock at night. If any of the crew, after that hour, still remained inclined for drinking, they were to do it on the open deck.
- That man that shall not keep his arms clean, fit for engagement, or neglect his business, shall be cut off from his share, and suffer such other punishment as the captain and the company shall think fit.
- If any man shall lose a joint in time of an engagement, shall have 400 pieces of eight: if a limb, 800.

- If at any time you meet with a prudent woman, that man that offers to meddle with her, without her consent, shall suffer present death.

Source: *The Way of the Pirate* by Robert Downie, pages 9 and 10.

Wow! They had to do their job, they went to bed early, they each had a vote, they knew what they were being paid, and they were not allowed to hit each other.

Questions to Ponder

Does your group have ground rules on how to treat each other that they have agreed to?

If not, when are you going to get this done?

This is a process thing, below the water level on that iceberg. Most groups will never do this and if you as a member or leader ask them to set ground rules, they will resist. It's too touchy-feely.

Until they talk about how they want to work together, they are all assuming that they know what everyone else thinks. That's a pretty big assumption.

If you take up the challenge and have your group establish ground rules, guess who gets to hold them accountable to those rules? Right! You, the leader! And don't expect them to like you for it, either. If you do take up this challenge and get them onboard, there will be huge dividends.

What would it be worth to have your team all driving toward the same goals (see "How Easy It Is to Assume") and working together as a team?

Cost of the flip chart paper: $20
Cost of the markers: $6
Having your team all on the same page and working together: priceless!

People support what they help create.

—J. Ogden Armour

ORIGIN OF A COMMON WORD

There is a myth that the origin of a certain word comes from the shipping of manure back to Europe when North America was in its colony stage. While the origin and use of this word predates colonial America, the mythical origin does have something to teach us about leadership.

Dried manure packaged in wooden boxes put into the leaky holds of those sailing ships would get wet and rehydrate. When that happened, it would also create methane gas down in those dark sealed holds.

Eventually a sailor was told to go check the cargo. When that sailor put the lantern down into the hold, the open flame and methane created an explosion that would burn the ship to the waterline. When they figured this out, the shipping companies began to re-label all the boxes of dried manure with a special designation: Ship High in Transit. You can guess why the myth about the origin of the word started.

Groups and organizations need to have the same concerns about creating an explosive situation. The danger isn't from methane gas but from all the unattended negative interactions between employees. This includes rumors, grudges, miscommunications, lack of teamwork, and more. If these issues are ignored, they will fester and create an explosive environment in your group, just like the manure creates methane gas.

The leader, or anyone else, has to be very careful about shedding light on the situation or else they will set it off. It is far better to ship high in transit and keep all those issues on the surface to begin with and not let them get a chance to fester.

Questions to Ponder

What is going on in your department that no one will talk about?

Why?

What do they have to do with what is really important to your group's success?

If they aren't critical to your group's success, how can you get the group focused on fixing the problem and not each other?

It's a rare person who wants to hear what he doesn't want to hear.

—Dick Cavett

REAL WORDS, REAL ORIGINS

average: A word of primarily nautical origin; possibly derived from the Arabic *awar*, **damaged goods**, and *awariya*, damages. The intermediate connection with English is probably the French *avarie*, customs duty (a twelfth-century usage). Its maritime usages included customs duties, extraordinary expenses of shipping damage at sea, and the equitable distribution of a resulting loss (the last still current in modern insurance practice). The modern mathematical sense, an arithmetic mean, occurs in English only. More loosely, the word has also come to mean ordinary, normal, typical, the common run of things.
(Source: *Ship to Shore* by Peter D. Jeans, page 12)

boss: To beat, Old High German *bozan*
(Source: *Why Do We Say It?* By Castle Books, page 44)

THE LITTLE BLUE PENGUINS

B ack in 2002, I had the opportunity to travel to Melbourne, Australia. I was there at the request of Eastman Kodak Company to train six of their supervisors for three weeks. It was an incredible experience for a number of reasons. Over the weekends, I had the time to look around and see some of the sights in that part of the world. One weekend I drove two hours from Melbourne to Phillip Island to see the Little Blue (a.k.a Fairy) Penguins Parade.

Walking in from the parking lot about a half hour before dusk, I noticed that I wasn't the only one interested in seeing the penguins. In fact, there were cement bleachers built on the beach to accommodate at least three to four hundred spectators, and they were filling up fast.

After a couple of minutes, the loudspeaker announced that the use of flash photography was strictly prohibited in at least three different languages. Then we waited for the sun to set. Then we waited some more.

Finally, there was some movement in the water. It was a penguin, a very small penguin. After a couple of minutes, there were more of them. Then one made its way up to the beach and stood up, then another and another. Eventually there were hundreds of them standing on the beach no farther than the highest waterline.

Every once in a while, some would dive back into the water. That went on for ten to twenty minutes. Fairy penguins would inch their way up to the beach's waterline only to dive back into the safety of the waves. Over and over again until finally, one made a break for it! That one penguin started a land rush. When one made the break, a bunch followed it across the beach and worked their way up to their roosts.

But they all didn't make it! If there was a gap and the next penguin to go didn't think they were close enough to the group, it would balk. When that penguin stopped, all the others stopped too. The whole process of diving back into the sea started all over again until the next brave little blue penguin started across and another bunch followed it across.

Wouldn't it be interesting to know if night after night it is the same penguins that make the break across the beach and lead the others? Maybe it is different penguins, who knows? Would you lead? Would you be the second across? What about in the first group, second? What makes the penguins stop and not follow the group across? No penguins were harmed in the creation or writing of this story, but the penguins have this waiting, diving-back-in, and rushing-the-beach behavior for a reason.

It's like our behavior in organizations. No one wants to take a risk but eventually, someone has to or the organization flounders. Who follows and backs up the risk, who doesn't and why? What happens in our organizations to people who do take risks? Are we breeding risk aversion in to our organizations and at what cost?

Questions to Ponder

What is the last risk you took at work?

What is the general risk-taking behavior at work?

What can you do to increase the amount of risks you and your coworkers are willing to take?

When will you start?

If you risk nothing, then you risk everything.

—Geena Davis

Security is mostly a superstition. It does not exist in nature, nor do the children of men as a whole experience it. Avoiding danger is no safer in the long run than outright exposure. Life is either a daring adventure or nothing.

—Helen Keller

WHO'S IN CHARGE?

On occasion, I go with my wife to conferences that she attends if the calendar works out and the event is in a good location. A while back, I went with her to a meeting in the summer in Vail, Colorado. It was an uneventful meeting, at least for me as the spouse, until the trip back from Vail to the Denver airport.

It is about a two-hour shuttle van ride back down the mountains to the airport. So we bummed our way into a friend's car. He had rented a subcompact and thought we could all fit in. It was a tight fit with our luggage and the five of us. But we did make it work. We figured it was still better than being stuck in the van.

About a half hour into the drive, we were coming downhill on the four-lane highway and saw the accident beginning to happen. Maybe a couple of hundred yards in front of us, a Winnebago towing a car breached up off the road like a whale in the ocean. Tires began squealing all around us and cars were pulling off the road and swerving to miss each other to avoid becoming part of a pileup. A huge eighteen-wheeler slammed on its brakes behind us and managed to avoid hitting anything! It was like Buzz Lightyear leading the toys across the street scene from the movie *Toy Story 2*. We looked around and everything and everybody had come to a stop. It was a miracle! That's when someone asked about the Winnebago and the cars in front of us. Should we go and see if we can help? Between the five of us, there were three surgeons, a surgical nurse, and my first aid card was expired so the answer was YES we should go help!

As we got near the site of the wreck, the three doctors each went in a different direction to see if they could help. Being reasonable with my expired first aid training, I decided to follow my wife. We worked our way to the Winnebago that was now lying on its side with all the front windows blown out. Lying on the front of the RV was an injured woman and another woman kneeling beside her taking care of her. As my wife came up to them, she asked if she could help. The woman who was kneeling said that she was a nurse and was taking care of it. My wife identified herself as a doctor. The nurse immediately briefed my wife as to what she had done and what she had found and asked, What do you want to do next, Doctor?

That was it! No discussion, no posturing about who was there first; it was an immediate acknowledgment of greater training and skill in that emergency situation. Not ten minutes later, the same thing happened again. Several emergency medical technicians (EMTs) were driving up the mountains and saw the accident. They had their equipment with them and came to help. Without exception when they identified themselves and their training, each and every doctor stepped back and said you know more about dealing with this type of situation than we do.

Questions to Ponder

Who is in charge?

Who do we listen to?

Whose input do we want?

Is it the person who has the highest rank, the person who is the loudest, or the person who's been trained the most for that situation?

How does your organization prepare to handle a busy crisis time?

Is it talked about before in the calm planning period or is it decided in the heat of the emergency?

What will you do if it all goes bad tomorrow?

Chance favors the prepared mind.

—Louis Pasteur

CHOIR JOE AND THE
LAUGHING SINGER

O ver the summers for the last decade or so, I have been fortunate to coordinate the leadership camps for the Western New York Rotary. These camps are aimed at high school and college-aged participants.

The success of these programs is due in large part to the quality of the presenters who come and bring their unique talents and perspectives to the participants. One of those presenters is Choir Joe. He has consistently been the highest rated presenter every time he comes. As you might guess from his name, he creates choirs with anybody he can!

Now these camps are about leadership, not music and certainly not about singing. Yet that is exactly what Joe does. His mission is to form these twenty to thirty people into a functioning choir in the course of an afternoon. He has the ability to take these participants and get them to do something they don't think they can do and they do it. Not only do they think they can't do it, they also don't want to do it (for the most part) and he still gets them to do it! At the end of the afternoon, the group sings and they sing well together in three-part harmony. It usually surprises the heck out of them. They can't believe that the sound they hear is coming from their own group.

This miracle of music happens but as you can easily imagine, sometimes there is resistance. As an experienced teacher, Joe is able to handle the typical methods of resistance with his charm and his ability to build confidence. There was this one time, though, when I saw an unusual method of resistance to Joe's teaching.

After about ten minutes of Joe's getting the students to begin singing, one student slowly and progressively began laughing. At first, it was just the uneasy laugh of "surely you don't expect us (me) to sing in public."

As the laughing escalated to the point where her whole body was shaking, her eyes began telling a story of deep fear. She couldn't stop herself. I watched her try but she couldn't. Looks from other participants and instructors couldn't stop her; she just kept laughing and laughing and laughing!

Along with the laughing, her eyes seemed to be asking her fellow participants to join her in her resistance as if to say, "Please join me and stop this from happening!" No one did; they just kept singing and working with Joe. Finally, she left the room to go to the rest room. Laughing can be a diuretic, right?

This was my chance to talk with her. I didn't think for a moment that she was laughing to be disruptive in any way, shape, or form purposely. She just couldn't help herself. At the same time, she was pulling, or trying to pull, the whole group down so she wouldn't be uncomfortable. That's what we talked about. She had a decision to make about whether to rejoin the group and not pull them down or to excuse herself from the activity. She chose to rejoin the group.

When we get uncomfortable, like when there are higher new expectations put on us, we have all sorts of behaviors to avoid it. Pulling the group down or keeping them from trying lets us stay in our comfort zone, but at what cost? If I'm uncomfortable and find some behavior to keep someone or ones from reaching their potential, that is sad! It happens all the time, but it is sad.

Expectations are going up all the time, people and groups are evolving; they must evolve to become and stay successful.

Questions to Ponder

How can you help individuals who might be scared and not let them block the rest of your group?

Where might that blocking be happening to you?

Where might it be happening in your group?

How can you work through or around it?

Origin of another word: confrontation

What does the word *confrontation* mean to you?

Is it a good thing, bad thing? Is it helpful to a group?

When I think of the word *confrontation*, I think of it in terms of a disagreement. Two or more people in a disagreement about what they believe or what they should do. The dictionary definition says that *confront* means "to face especially in challenge: oppose" (*Webster's New Collegiate Dictionary*).

In a group situation this can be a problem. We do want confrontation in our groups because as General George S. Patton said, "If everyone is thinking alike, then somebody isn't thinking."

We don't want conflict, but we need confrontation. The word *confront* originally meant something a little different. It came from two words *con* and *front* from Latin.

con: With
front: To face

Originally, *confront* meant "to face with not oppose."

As leaders, we want to guide our groups back to the original meaning of the word.

Questions to Ponder

Listen to what's being said at the next meeting you go to.
Are there sides to whatever topic is being discussed?

Are the different sides trying to win favor for their ideas?

Is there a difference in opinion?

Why?

How are they facing the same problem together, or are they facing each other?

What is your group confronting, the goal or problem or each other?

What can you do to get them focused on the main thing?

When will you start?

Section 3

Planning and Solving Skills

Confucius said, "Those whose paths are not the same do not consult one another."
—([15:40] from *The Essential Confucius* by Thomas Cleary)

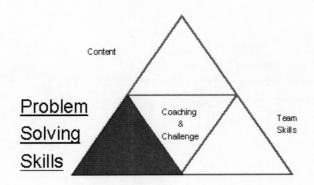

WHAT'S THE ANSWER?

H ere's a challenge I have used for a number of years.
Imagine that the bottle below is real. You pick up the key, remove the cork, and put the key into the bottle. Now recork the bottle. The key is in and the bottle is sealed.

Here's the problem: You want that key out. There are a couple of rules you need to work around, though. First, you cannot break the bottle. Second, you cannot pull the cork out of the bottle.

Write down what pops into your mind. Record your thinking as you go through the process of solving the problem. I'll wait while you do that.

Okay, finished? Go to page 76 and read the section labeled Bottle and Key Problem.

> The "Feynman Problem Solving Algorithm"
>
> 1. write down the problem;
> 2. think very hard;
> 3. write down the answer.
>
> *Richard Phillips Feynman*

BLIND MEN AND THE ELEPHANT (A.K.A. "BLIND MEN")

(by John Godfrey Saxe)

American poet John Godfrey Saxe (1816-1887) based this poem, "The Blind Men and the Elephant," on a fable that was told in India many years ago. It is a good warning about how our sensory perceptions can lead to misinterpretations.

It was six men of Indostan

To learning much inclined,
Who went to see the Elephant
(Though all of them were blind),
That each by observation
Might satisfy his mind

The First approached the Elephant,
　　And happening to fall
Against his broad and sturdy side,
　　At once began to bawl:
"God bless me! but the Elephant
　　Is very like a wall!"

The Second, feeling of the tusk,
　　Cried, "Ho! what have we here
So very round and smooth and sharp?
　　To me 'tis mighty clear
This wonder of an Elephant
　　Is very like a spear!"

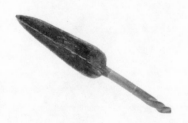

The Third approached the animal,
　　And happening to take
The squirming trunk within his hands,
　　Thus boldly up and spake:
"I see," quoth he, "the Elephant
　　Is very like a snake!"

The Fourth reached out an eager hand,
    And felt about the knee.
"What most this wondrous beast is like
    Is mighty plain," quoth he;
"'Tis clear enough the Elephant
    Is very like a tree!"

The Fifth, who chanced to touch the ear,
    Said: "E'en the blindest man
Can tell what this resembles most;
    Deny the fact who can
This marvel of an Elephant
    Is very like a fan!"

The Sixth no sooner had begun
    About the beast to grope,
Than, seizing on the swinging tail
    That fell within his scope,
"I see," quoth he, "the Elephant
    Is very like a rope!"

And so these men of Indostan
    Disputed loud and long,
Each in his own opinion
    Exceeding stiff and strong,
Though each was partly in the right,
    And all were in the wrong!

Moral:

So oft in theologic wars,
    The disputants, I ween,
Rail on in utter ignorance
    Of what each other mean,
And prate about an Elephant
    Not one of them has seen!

Questions to Ponder

What more needs to be said?

If we don't listen to other perspectives when planning and solving, we will never have the whole picture!

Leaders lead the group to listen to each other even when they don't want to, even when they think they don't need to.

Some will never learn anything because they understand everything too soon.

—Thomas Blount

OUTSMARTING SQUIRRELS

A friend of mine, Tom Murphy, lives in the woods of Vermont. His deck has several bird feeders lining the perimeter. As is often the case, the squirrels have made these bird feeders a favorite feeding spot whenever the feeders are filled.

In the summer of 2007, Tom was getting frustrated with the squirrels taking advantage of his generosity and emptying the feeders before the birds even had a chance. He struck upon a plan to keep the plucky squirrels from climbing the pole to get to the birdseed. He decided to paint the pole!

Not fifteen minutes after the job was completed and the bird feeder filled, the first squirrel showed up. Tom was pleased to see the squirrel struggle with the painted pole. He took great delight in seeing the squirrel not only unable to climb the pole and steal the feed but get covered with all that fresh, wet, slippery paint.

Then the plan took an unexpected turn. The freshly painted squirrel began running all over his deck, leaving a trail of painted squirrel prints in its wake!

Every solution creates new and perhaps unforeseen problems. Before launching a new solution, it is always beneficial to consider what potential problems might be created or developed. You still might implement the solution but at least you considered and are hopefully better prepared for those new problems!

Questions to Ponder

The next time you or your group is about to make a decision, do a PMI by asking the following questions.

1. If we take this option, what are the positive outcomes we can reasonably expect?   Positive
2. If we take this option, what are the negative outcomes we can reasonably expect?   Minus
3. If we take this option, what are the interesting options that are neither positive nor negative that we can expect?   Interesting

It is far less for lack of intelligence, than for lack of method, that men achieve less than they desire.

Anonymous

BOTTLE AND KEY PROBLEM

What did you write? Anything? When I present this exercise in a workshop, the group always goes right to solutions. These ideas are recorded on a flip chart. Typical ideas are as follows: push the cork in, cut the bottle, cut the cork, burn the cork, drill a hole in the bottle, get another key.

What ideas did you come up with? Did you define the problem first to get it clear in your mind? That would mean writing down the rules and the goal again: can't pull the cork out and can't break the bottle, get that key out. It also means writing down any other information about the problem you know about or can observe.

In my workshops after we look at the flip chart of ideas, I ask the group to slow down and define the problem. At this point, they observe that in addition to the rules and the goals, the problem also involves a bottle made of glass, a cork, a metal key, and air. Air! When someone says air, there is usually a little laugh shared by the group.

For the most part that hadn't occurred to them, they defined it as a group. That's powerful!

More information about the problem means that when they do go to the next step of generating options, they know more and can generate more options. Options equal power! The more options you and your group have in any situation, the more power they have.

If one person in the group generates an additional idea because they learned one additional fact, that might set up a cascade of new ideas. That one additional idea might lead to someone else coming up with an idea that would never have occurred to them and so on throughout the entire group. By slowing down to define the problem, the goal, and what we each know about it, we can exponentially increase the idea generating and therefore the problem-solving power of the group. It is more than worth the effort to slow down and define the problem!

Questions to Ponder

Where might your group be jumping to solutions?

What have you and your group done to define the parameters of the problem?

the main criteria for success

the current status of those criteria

the budget available

the personnel available

the amount of time until you have to have a solution

When are you going to get started?

I had six honest serving men:
They taught me all I knew.
Their names were where and what and when and why and how
and who.

—Kipling

One is only properly motivated to achieve a goal when he is able
to define it.

—W. J. Reddin

LIVING BELOW
OUR POTENTIAL

C reativity consultant Roger von Oech estimates that the average person takes over 2,600 tests, quizzes, and exams through the formal years of training. What does this teach us about making mistakes? My guess is that we learn to avoid them. We all want that "A" to put on our refrigerator door. In school, we have to face those tests and work through the hard stuff we want to avoid. After we leave school, though, that becomes more of a choice. How do we continue to challenge ourselves? What do we choose to take on that we don't have to? What is our starting premise? The answers to those questions greatly determine our ultimate success in life. Do we avoid taking on something because we think it will be difficult? If we do that, then we may never find our real potential or anything close to our real potential. So do we start with the premise that it might be hard but we are smart enough to figure it out, or do we start with the premise that it's too difficult, so why bother? If we choose the former, we begin to take on problems and tasks and overcome them and we may get a glimpse at our potential. If we choose the former: we stay safe in our own little world while the rest of the world changes and we will never know just what we might have been capable of.

Borrowing a term from Steve Faber seek out those "OSM!s" (Oh Shit Moments!), put yourself out there every once in a while. See what you're capable of; it can be fun to surprise yourself and maybe others.

Questions to Ponder

Where are you holding yourself back because you might fail?

What would happen if you did fail, really?

What is likely to happen if you don't find a safe solution to that issue?

Which is riskier, taking the risk or not doing anything?

When are you going to get started?

A lot of people are afraid to say what they want. That's why they don't get what they want.

—Madonna

To win without risk is to triumph without glory.

—Pierre Corneille

TESTING ASSUMPTIONS

My oldest brother raised three sons. The three of them were about six years apart. Between the three of them, there were the typical challenges. As teenagers they would push the envelope to see what they could do and get away with.

One of my nephews, Mikie, the youngest, wanted to get an earring. His father had been pretty clear that he didn't want to see his sons wearing an earring in his house and that he would remove it. Mikie was undaunted and against his older brothers' advice wore his new post home.

When Dad got home from work that day, all the boys were there to see what would happen. It only took a few minutes for the new earring to be spotted. Dad calmly walked over to his son, pinched the post between his index finger and thumb, and pulled it straight down!

Mikie grabbed his ear! His brothers ran over to him to see if he was all right. Mikie started to laugh, stood up, and let go of his ear. Amazingly, his ear wasn't injured and there wasn't a drop of blood!

The reason? He was smart enough to use a magnetic earring. His ear wasn't pierced; he just had the earring held on by a magnet in the back of his earlobe. He was testing to see what exactly was going to happen if he did get his ear pierced. Now he knew!

What would you like to do but the potential bad result is holding you back? How can you find out by testing just how bad, or not so bad, the perceived outcome might be without risking the real consequence? In the case of Mikie's earring, there was the added benefit of everyone, including my brother, bursting up and laughing about it. As far as I know, Mikie still doesn't have his ear pierced. He may still have that magnetic post, though!

Questions to Ponder

What assumptions have you and or your group been living with?

What can you do to test those assumptions?

Only those who risk going too far can possibly find out how far they can go.

—T. S. Eliot

Section 4

Challenge and Coaching Skills

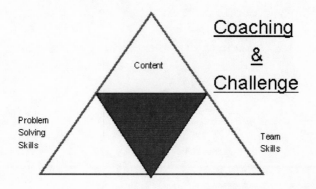

STEEL MILLS, BROOMSTICKS, AND THERMOSTATS

The summer between my junior and senior year in college, I was fortunate enough to get a job at a steel mill near my hometown of McDonald, Ohio. This was during the 1970s, and the mills in that area of the country were still working and paying well. I was fortunate to be one of the first hires that summer. Beyond the paycheck, I learned a lot of valuable life lessons over those three and a half months.

After three months working in the mill, you became a union member. That meant that the first group of us hired would be there long enough to join. As a union member, you were no longer considered a summer replacement and could, if you wanted to, stay on and continue to work at the mill. Some of the guys did do exactly that and I'm sure they put away some great money. What I don't know is if they ever used that to go back to school.

During those first three months, before you were a union member, we were required to wear black and yellow stripes on our helmets. These stripes told everyone you were not a union member. They also announced that you were a college student on summer break and didn't know what you were doing. This opened the door, for me, to a valuable leadership lesson on challenging the group norms.

Jobs in the mill were assigned by seniority. Being the newest hired meant you had very few choices. I was assigned to one of the shipping areas as a sweeper. I swept out the lunchrooms, the offices, and any other area the foreman told me to sweep. I quickly figured out that there were only so many areas to sweep and that the foreman had a lot to do and wasn't interested in keeping me busy. That meant the sooner I got all my sweeping done the sooner I could do something else or relax. It was the something else that got me into a little bit of hot water with my coworkers.

They noticed that I was hanging around and asking them questions every afternoon about what they were doing. I just wanted to figure out how the mill worked and what their jobs were. They began telling me the same phrase over and over: "Slow down, college boy, we're not setting any records here today!" Over the next week or so they kept telling me that, but I guess I didn't get it: I was just interested in what they were doing.

Finally, while I was on break, someone broke my broom. The shorter broomstick made my job harder and clearly conveyed the message that I needed to slow down. The guys had gotten their message across to me, the eager college student, that they didn't want me to work too fast. If I finished the job that fast, then that would set an expectation of how long the job should take. They knew that when I left, one of them would have to sweep and they didn't want to work that fast. This was the first but not the only time I saw and experienced this pattern of behavior in the mill or since.

Today, I think about this and how it is like a thermostat. The thermostats in our offices and houses are error activated. If the temperature gets too cold, that registers on the thermostat as an error and sends a message to the furnace to turn on and heat the room back up a certain temperature. When that happens, the thermostat sends a message to the furnace that the error has been corrected and it sends the signal to the furnace to shut off. If the temperature in the room gets too warm, the same thing happens. Only this time the signal is sent to the air conditioner to cool the room down below a set temperature.

That is exactly what happened to me in the steel mill when I was sweeping too fast! My behavior registered as an error in the group. It was outside the group's comfort zone. My behavior then set in play a series of corrective behaviors by the group to get me back within their comfort zone, not too fast and not too slow. Groups have their comfort zones and behaviors to keep the situation within parameters. Just like the thermostatic system with the furnace and air conditioner, our human systems will exaggerate our corrective behaviors to get the situation back within our comfort zones.

As leaders, we need to reset those comfort zones. We cannot accept the status quo. Our job as leaders is to challenge the status quo and do better. That means we are likely to run into behaviors from our teams that will resist our efforts to do better. Without a challenge, our team, any team, has no reason to be better or to produce better results. This is the essence of being a leader, we have to challenge them or we will just get more of the status quo.

Expect some challenging behaviors from your group as you challenge them. You may be doing exactly what has to be done for the group to succeed and yet get resistance from them. They are likely to exaggerate their behavior to get you back into their comfort zone before they give it up.

Questions to Ponder

What process or function in your department or group has gotten too comfortable, too easy?

When was the last time your group really had to rally together to meet a difficult challenge?

Around what process or function can you challenge your group by asking, How might we . . . ?

When will you do this?

There isn't a person anywhere who isn't capable of doing more than he thinks he can.

—Henry Ford

LEADING THE WAY
THEY NEED TO BE LED

B eginners need specific directions.
     A while ago while teaching in Vermont, I found my favorite example of how to lead a beginner. The story was a gift that came out of a workshop I was teaching, and it has become my standard.

In my leadership workshop, it is pretty typical to find out who, if anyone, attending has served in the military. In this particular class, two men raised their hands. From there I begin to ask them a series of questions about their experience:

—How old were you when you entered the military?
—How pleasant was that first conversation with your drill instructor?
—How well did you know how to make a bed?
—What role did a quarter play in your learning how to make a bed?
—How well did you know how to take care of your own personal hygiene, like brushing your teeth and shaving?

This is where it got interesting. One of the guys thought about it for a minute and then answered, "Well, they did make us cover the bristles on the toothbrush but once it got into your mouth then it was up to you as to how you brushed them."

At this point, the other gentleman scoffed, "It must have been the army!" Well, that's just too good of a comment for me to leave alone so I asked him what he meant by that. His answer was that not only had he been in the United States Marine Corps but that he was a drill instructor.

"Wow! You were a DI?" I responded. He quickly corrected me. "No, there was only one DI, and that was Jack Webb. I was a drill instructor."

Discretion being the better part of valor, I let that one go and veered the conversation back to brushing your teeth. The sergeant was clear that in the Marines it was not up to you. Those teeth are still Marine Corps property. The appropriate procedure is "Up down, up down, up down, switch, until all four quadrants of your mouth were covered. At that point I would then have the men chew a tablet and personally inspect each mouth looking for tartar."

What a beautiful example of specific directions to help a beginner succeed! There are precise directions, the leader is there to ensure proper implementation, and the leader has a very specific level of performance that is measured.

Regardless of a person's resume and what they might tell you about their experience until you see them perform the task, job, whatever, you really don't know what their skills are.

How often on the job do we ask if someone can handle a job and then leave them alone to do it? There's a lot to be done so we have no other choice, right? I'm not so sure about that. If the job isn't done right, will there be time to do it over? Isn't that the joke? How come there is always time to do it over but not the time to do it right in the first place?

Doing it right means that the person who does know how to do the job stays there and teaches step by step how to do it right instead of coming back five days, hours, or even minutes later to discover a mess.

Taking the time to be with someone to teach them does take time. Does it take more time than fixing mistakes? Maybe! Does it take more time than fixing that person's mistake after that, and the next one, and the next one? Probably not.

What about the damage that is done? How excited are you to take on a job knowing that if you don't do it right your boss will charge in and fix it but didn't take the time to teach you how to do it in the first place or even to give you a clear standard of performance? My guess is, not very.

If you haven't seen a person do a job, you are taking your chances. The fact that abandoning beginners works every once in a while isn't a validation that it is a good leadership style. You were just lucky because they were bright enough to figure it out. But what about next time, what about all your other employees? You may be giving up on a lot of talent because you don't want to spend the time up front to teach them the right way from the beginning.

Questions to Ponder

Who in your group is struggling?

What is their competency to do the job? Have they ever performed it at a high level? An acceptable level? At all? If they have never performed the skills of the job well, then this is a training issue.

If they have performed the task well in the past, what is their confidence level now? If they have performed well in the past and they are struggling somehow now, it's a confidence issue. Build their confidence.

If they have not performed the job well on their own in the past and their confidence is low, then it is both a training-and-confidence-building project for you.

When are you going to start?

Be not afraid of going slowly, be only afraid of standing still.
                                                    —Chinese proverb

Never discourage anyone . . . who continually makes progress, no matter how slow.
                                                    —Plato

THE DANGLE DUO

Getting People Invested

While living in Vermont in the 1980s, I learned about ropes courses. These experiential activities have a rich potential to teach us about how we make decisions, work together in groups, and take on challenges. Many of the games and activities are played on the ground, but some are done in the trees while being belayed. Anytime participants are asked to climb a ladder or tree, they should be belayed by wearing a harness attached to a rope. At the other end of the rope is an experienced instructor who, on a moment's notice, pulls in and holds on to the rope to avoid any potential of a fall.

Part of becoming an instructor for me was to learn how to tie the appropriate knots and to trust the belay system. My instructor Paul tricked me into learning these lessons by inviting me out to the ropes course one Saturday on a pretense. He told me that he had a new high ropes element that he wanted to test out and asked if I would help.

When I got to the site, there were three other people in addition to Paul. The two newbies, myself, and another person were asked to put on our climbing harnesses because we were going to try out the dangle duo.

The dangle duo looks like a huge free-swinging ladder suspended from a crossbar between two trees. The rungs of the ladder, though, are six-foot-long poles that are a good four inches in diameter. The other nice touch to the dangle duo is that the rungs get progressively farther apart and therefore harder to climb as they get higher off the ground.

Once we had our harnesses on, we were instructed to tie a very specific knot, the bowline on a bite. Tied correctly it makes a very nice double rope loop to connect to your harness. Tied incorrectly and it makes a slipknot that will get tighter and tighter as it takes on weight.

After we were instructed how to tie the knot, we practiced a couple of times and then headed over to the dangle duo. About twenty feet off the ground and a good ten minutes into our climb, we both had a revelation. We both realized that we had tied our own knots. There were a few minutes of panicked discussion: Did the instructors check them before we started to climb? Had we double-checked them ourselves before climbing? Were they tied correctly and not slipknots? With both our hearts working overtime, we called down to Paul and the other instructor to ask if our belay knots were okay. Paul's answer was "You tied them, what do you think?"

We had both just assumed that our instructors would check them to be sure, which I'm sure they did, but they wanted us to be sure. Now we had to check them again for ourselves while depending on them twenty feet in the air. To our relief both knots were tied correctly and we continued our climb and were eventually lowered to the ground by the ropes with our knots tied in them.

The experience of climbing the dangle duo and depending on a knot that I tied myself was a lesson in getting people invested in success. With a lot personally on the line, literally, I was totally committed to tying a perfect knot.

From that point, I was a lot more careful about tying knots and diligent about checking them before anyone got off the ground.

Questions to Ponder

Looking at the people in your department, are they more vested in their personal success or the department's success?

How can those two become more in alignment?

How can you get others in your department to experience what it is like to use, and depend upon, the service or product they produce?

Few things can help an individual more than to place responsibility on him, and to let him know that you trust him.
—Booker T. Washington

Duties constrain managers, objectives liberate them.
—W. J. Reddin

THE BLOODY PAPER

Keep Your Standards High

D r. Len Bosari taught family systems theory at Springfield College in the early 1980s. In the fall of 1980, I took Len's class. My expectation of that class was to get an A and not much else. I wasn't married, I didn't have any children, and I wasn't even in a relationship at the time. It was just another academic experience I had to go through.

None of that mattered to Len and I'm sure I wasn't even on his radar screen as a student. At least not until the first paper when we became well acquainted. My paper came back looking like he had cut himself shaving. Red marks were everywhere. It was an ugly mess and I was really embarrassed. So I did what I normally did when I didn't connect with a teacher: I went and tried to use my glowing personality and schmoozed him.

To say that my tactic didn't work is an understatement. He held firm and I was getting desperate when he began asking me questions about the paper like, "What did you mean by this? Where have you seen this before?" He was coaching me. That was good; even if the grade stood for this paper, maybe I could salvage my grade yet. My next paper wasn't quite the arterial gusher that the first one was, but it was still a mess. At this point in the term, we were beyond the add-drop date so I was committed to the class and couldn't get out. So it was off to see Len for another coaching session. He didn't hesitate and went right back to asking questions and coaching me to write a better paper. I'm not the quickest study so I visited Len before and after every paper from that point on. He was persistent and by the end of the term, I actually wrote a paper that he liked. I had finally earned my "A" grade.

Len was teaching family systems theory, but he taught me an important lesson in leadership that probably wasn't on the class curriculum. The

lesson was leaders should never, never, never lower our standards. At the
same time, we cannot abandon our responsibility as leaders and teachers.
As leaders, we must commit ourselves to bringing performance up to
the standards or expectations. That means spending time coaching and
building both skill and confidence.

Len did that for me. It was a masterful lesson in leadership!

Questions to Ponder

Where has your group gotten complacent?

What standards have slipped for you or your group?

How can you reawaken the challenge for yourself or your group
to perform at a higher level?

We are what we repeatedly do. Excellence, then, is not an act
but a habit.

—Aristotle

THE SLIGHT EDGE

T hink you can't be successful, really successful, because you don't have the talent of other people? Well, maybe you could develop your skill and get better, but that would take a lot of hard work? And to get the benefits of that hard work you would have to get a lot better, right? Maybe not!

Small improvements in performance can make huge differences over time. The key isn't huge differences in skill or talent. It's being just a little bit better, consistently, over time.

Take a look at this example from the 2006 PGA statistics and how much better Tiger Woods was compared to the other golfers.

PGA 2006 Scoring Average Statistics & Money Leaders (Source: PGA.com)

#1 @ 68.11 strokes/round = Tiger Woods—$9,941,563
#2 @ 68.86 strokes/round = Jim Furyk—$7,213,316
#3 @ 68.95 s/r = Adam Scott—$4,978,858
#51 @ 70.67 s/r = Charles Warren—$1,018,840 (#92)

Tiger Woods was 2.56 strokes better per round, on average, than Charles Warren and that translated to $8,922,723 more income over that year!

Tiger Woods was only .75 strokes better per round, on average than the number 2 golfer in the world in 2006, Jim Furyk. On the basis of that slight edge, Tiger Woods made an extra $2,728,247 more income in that one year!

In addition to those statistics, add this:

> Tiger Woods played fifteen events in 2006
> Jim Furyk played twenty-four
> Charles Warren played twenty-seven

You can see that Tiger wasn't a lot better; he was just a little bit better consistently. Less than three strokes per round of 18 holes made the difference between being the number 51 golfer in the world and number 1. The slight edge created almost $9 million more in income and allowed Tiger Woods to play in twelve less tournaments than Charles Warren.

Being just a little bit better allowed him to play in fewer tournaments and to win a lot more money than anyone else. What might you be just a little bit better at consistently for the next year?

Questions to Ponder

What is one key task that you perform almost daily?

What can you do to be just a little better at it for the next three months?

What key task can your group do just a little better at for the next three months?

To improve is to change; to be perfect is to change often.
—Winston Churchill

No Guarantees

The last full time job I had was as the director of the Church Street
Center at the University of Vermont. The Church Street Center
was UVM's non-credit community education offering. We offered one-week
to eight-week informational classes on a wide variety of topics like cooking,
personal growth, computers, just about anything we thought there might
be an audience for. Since none of these classes carried college credit, we
didn't have any limitations on what we could offer.

It was an exciting opportunity to direct this program. It was a chance
to be creative, learn about marketing, and to continue to develop my
leadership skills. When I took the job, the department wasn't in the best
of shape and morale was low.

So I launched myself in to the job and began using a lot of the skills
and stories relayed in this book. I painted the picture of the Church Street
Center as a beautiful three-masted schooner. It had the potential to be
beautiful, but the sails were ripped, the workings in disrepair, and there
was a huge hole in the hull. We couldn't put into port to fix it, and it didn't
make much sense to start by polishing the brass: we had to fix the holes
in the hull first.

So we got to work, I met with the staff and we set our priorities, we
figured out what needed to be done, and we got busy. Each week we would
meet and assess where we were and what we needed to do next. I tried very
hard to paint that picture of the schooner and keep a positive outlook as
the situation improved.

There were the normal fits and starts that happen when building any
team, but overall as a group, we made steady progress and started working
together better. A couple of months into the job, there was a test. I pushed
hard for a particular cover design for our catalog but the group lined
up against me and overruled me. Well, I let them overrule me. I could

have pulled rank but I had been talking about making shared decisions. I couldn't convince them I was right so I didn't have any valid reason other than because "I'm the boss!" to base my decision. There are those times when we need to listen to the group, and I decided this was one of them. After that, the group seemed to pick up energy and motivation. We had some good discussions about what was best for the department and our numbers improved.

Then it happened! Nine months into the job, I got a monthly financial report from Tara, our financial assistant that I didn't understand. So I wandered over to her cubicle to ask her to explain it to me. What I found out later was that a previous supervisor had done this same thing only to embarrass her in front of other employees. Tara wasn't going to fall for this trick again. When I asked my question, she exploded like a cat on a dog's face. We were in an open room in cubicles. She was yelling at me for questioning her competency. What went through my mind at that moment was "What does everyone think I said to her to set her off like this?" Needless to say, I was embarrassed for both of us. What could I do? If I tried to interrupt her, she'd get madder and probably wouldn't listen to a thing I said. I knew I hadn't done anything bad enough to set her off like this but, boy, was she mad! So I let her go. It took a while but when she finished, I apologized for anything I might have done and said that I really needed her help to understand what the report said. I told her I didn't know who else to ask and if she could help me.

That worked. If it hadn't, I don't know what I would have done. As I said, I found out she was, in her mind, defending herself from an attack. Despite the fact that we had worked together for nine months and she had never seen nor heard of me doing anything remotely like that. She had been hurt by a previous supervisor and she wasn't going to be treated badly again.

We got by that and talked about it. I'm happy to say it didn't happen again while I was at the Church Street Center. I had assumed that all the issues were out on the table and the group trusted me. I was wrong. For nine-plus months, that issue sat out there with Tara like methane in a ship's hold. When I opened the hatch, it went off!

Questions to Ponder

What might you be assuming about the trust in your group?

When your group fights, do they fight about what's right for the department or what they do to each other? In other words, are the fights about the main thing or only about surface issues?

What can you do to test and deepen the trust in your group?

When?

A man should never be ashamed to own he has been in the wrong, which is but saying in other words that he is wiser today than he was yesterday.

—Pape

Eighty percent of success is showing up.

—Woody Allen

Experience is an asset of which no worker can be cheated, no matter how selfish or greedy his immediate employer may be.

—Napoleon Hill

Section 5

Now What

I f you've made it this far, you might be wondering how to get started. This last section of the book is a basic outline of how to get started in a group that you inherited, just joined, or are just starting. The process below is a combination of some classic group facilitation tools including the nominal group technique and the force field analysis.

SET GROUP GROUND RULES

Just as the pirates were smart enough to set their group's ground rules before setting sail, it is a good idea for our modern-day groups to do the same. Expect resistance to this step. This may seem like another touchy-feely exercise to some of the more cynical members of your group. When you take this step, the worst thing you can do is to make those cynics right. Once you start down this path as a leader, you have to go all the way. What I mean by this is that you, as the leader, have to follow through and enforce whatever ground rules they come up with. If you don't, you will be guilty of rubber lipping and the cynics would have been correct. It would have been a touchy-feely group exercise.

Before your meeting to set ground rules, it would be a good idea to brief your group on your expectations. Let them know that you want them to come to the meeting prepared to list how they want the group to behave toward each other. If they ask why, it is easy to explain that it is much easier to have the conversation when the group is not burdened with the primary task of reaching the goal and not unduly stressed. Again, whatever ground rules they come up with, follow them. Once you start using these rules and holding the group accountable to follow them, they can always adjust, change, add, or adapt them as they see fit. They are always the group's rules, not the leader's rules although you can add yours to the list.

The process of generating the group's ground rules is relatively simple. With the group assembled and with a flip chart, go around the room and get one rule or positive behavior from each member of the group. Try to keep the rules positive and not negative. So instead of having a ground rule about no interrupting, it might be reworded to say, "We let each person finish his or her thought." This will make holding the group accountable to these rules a more positive experience. Continue circling around the group until everyone passes and the group is satisfied that the list is complete.

That list should be printed and distributed to each member of the group for approval and for them to bring with them to all subsequent meetings. It is vital that they all, at least verbally, agree to these ground rules. A copy of the group's ground rules could also be reproduced on a large pad of paper to display at every meeting. At first, it will be the leader's job, in all likelihood, to hold the group accountable to these rules. Over time, your goal is to encourage any member of the group to do the same.

WHAT HAS TO HAPPEN AROUND HERE

O ne of the first things you will need to do if you are taking over an established group is to get a sense of what they do and what competencies they need to be good at. This will help you get up to speed and to begin equipping you to determine how they are performing. Doing a time flowchart of what happens in the organization is helpful. In this meeting, or series of meetings, you and the group lay out what happens in chronological order from the first contact or request for service/product with a client all the way through to the last step.

This process is helpful in a number of ways. First, it will allow you and the whole group to get a sense of what all those steps are. Sometimes individuals are only aware of the steps to a process immediately before and after their own. Secondly, this process will allow you and the group to assess who does what and clarify that point. If that sounds odd, consider that tasks performed by someone who has the responsibility to do it but not the authority can lead to trouble. Without both responsibility and authority to do a job, there can easily be a lack of ownership. Without ownership the task is not likely to be done well. On top of that, for the leader, how can you hold someone accountable to doing a good job if he/she is not given the authority to make it happen? A third benefit from doing this time flow process is that you and the group can look for efficiencies and overlaps to shorten the process.

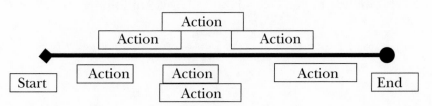

107

TOP PRIORITIES

B rief your group to come to the priority meeting prepared to list out the top measures of success for your organization or department. You are looking for the quantifiable or describable characteristics that would be proof that your organization or department was doing really well. Each member of your team needs to come prepared to list out from their perspective what those top criteria are.

At this meeting, a nominal group technique works well. Just as before, you can go around the table one person at a time and record their answers on a flip chart. This process continues until the whole group is satisfied that all the measures are listed.

For the next step, review the list to combine any similar items and to clarify any terms that are not understood. With that completed, each person present is given five votes. Each person can vote for one item five times or split their five votes any way they see fit. No discussion or bargaining is allowed. Following the voting process, the group can take a break while you and another person tallies the votes.

Usually there is a natural break point between the top-vote getters and the rest of the pack. As tempting as it might be, the group cannot work on all the criteria that received votes. Determine the top tier of priorities and limit the group's focus to these measures for the rest of the process. A top tier of anywhere between four and six main measures is good. Any less than three and the group might be putting too many eggs in to few baskets. Any more than six and they might be diluting their efforts.

WHERE ARE WE NOW?

B rief your group to come to this meeting prepared to list out anything and everything they can think of to quantify and qualify in as much detail as they can to describe the current situation for one, and only one, of the top measures of success. This process is repeated for each of the top measures of success.

At this meeting, all the descriptors of the current situation are recorded. If someone says it is a descriptor, it is recorded on the flip chart without discussion. This process continues until the whole group is satisfied that they have a complete description of the current situation for that particular measure of success.

All the information generated in this meeting, as for all of these meetings, should be recorded on paper and distributed to each member of the group. This will keep the group on target, focused on the same information, and provide a record of their progress.

Now

WHERE DO WE WANT TO BE?

B rief your group to come to this meeting prepared to list out anything and everything they can think of to quantify and qualify an ideal state for one specified measure of success. They should be ready to describe where they want to be if they are successful. This process is repeated for each of the top measures of success.

At this meeting, all the descriptors of the ideal situation are recorded. If someone says it is a descriptor, it is recorded on the flip chart without discussion. This process continues until the whole group is satisfied that they have a complete description of the ideal situation for that particular measure of success.

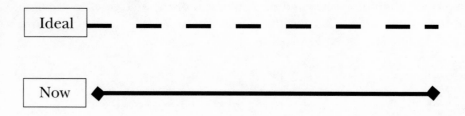

What's Helping?

Brief your group to come to this meeting prepared to list out anything and everything they can think of that is helping them, and the rest of the organization, to move closer to the ideal state they described earlier. They should be ready to describe all those little, big, and in-between behaviors; initiatives; efforts; rules and regulations; anything that is having a positive influence in moving the measure of success toward the ideal level. This process is repeated for each of the top measures of success.

At this meeting, all the drivers moving the group in the direction of the ideal are recorded. If you prefer, you can have the members of the group each have a stack of index cards. Each person writes one driver per card. Provide as many index cards as they need. For clarity of the process, it is best to have one color for this step and a different color for the next step. The reason for that will be clarified later.

Once the group has finished their individual work writing down the drivers, they are ready for the next step. At this point, they can gather around a big table and start announcing their individual drivers and placing their cards on the table. Any one with a similar driver adds their card to create a pile. This can be validating for the group in that they begin to see that they are thinking alike. If there are drivers that are not similar to any other generated by the group, that is validating too. Instead of difference in thinking being a roadblock to success in the group, it becomes a positive one. If that one person were not a member of the group, then that information would not be available to them. More information at this stage means the group will have a more complete picture of the drivers. That increases the group's power. So thinking differently is encouraged to make the group more powerful.

This process continues until all the drivers are out on the table. For now the main groupings should be recorded. The individual cards should be kept for a later step in the process. Again, this process is repeated for each separate main measure of success.

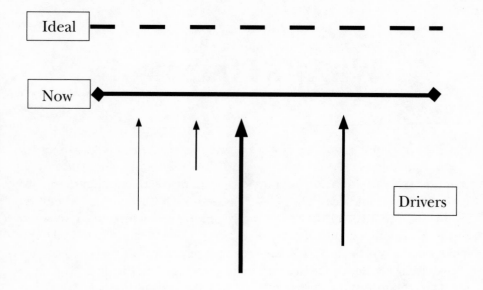

WHAT'S BLOCKING

B rief your group to come to this meeting prepared to list out anything and everything they can think of that is blocking or hindering them, and the rest of the organization, to move closer to the ideal state they described earlier. They should be ready to describe all those little, big, and in-between behaviors; initiatives; efforts; rules and regulations; anything that is having a negative or blocking influence in moving the measure of success toward the ideal level. This process is repeated for each of the top measures of success.

At this meeting, all the inhibitors blocking or slowing progress to move the measure of success in the direction of the ideal are recorded. Again, if you prefer, give each member of the group a stack of index cards to write one inhibitor per card. It is important to write the inhibitors on a different colored index card than the drivers.

Once the group has finished their individual work writing down the inhibitors, they are ready for the next step. At this point, they again gather around a big table and start announcing their individual blockers and placing them out on the table. Any similar inhibitors are grouped to create a pile.

This process continues until all the inhibitors are out on the table. For now, the main groupings should be recorded. The individual cards should be kept for a later step in the process. Again, this process is repeated for each separate main measure of success.

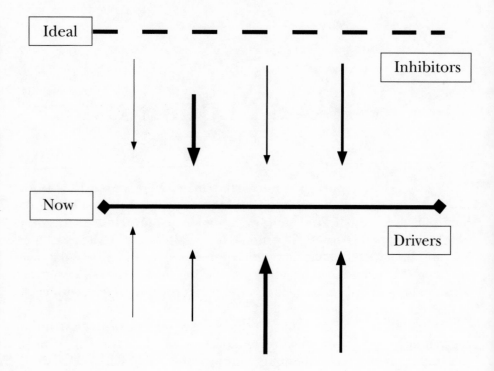

WHAT DO WE CONTROL?

Brief your group to come to this meeting or meetings prepared to discuss how much control they have on each individual driver and inhibitor.

At the meeting, the group gathers around a large table. On the table, you can have a prepared large sheet of paper with a large bull's-eye drawn on it. The "A" innermost circle represents what the group has control over. The next "B" outer circle is where they have influence, and the third or "C" circle represents the area of no control.

Taking each driver and inhibitor one at a time, the group now assigns them to one of the three spheres of control. At the end of this process, because drivers and inhibitors are on different color cards it is still clear which they represent.

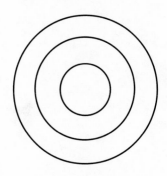

A: Inner Circle = Control
B: Second Circle = Influence
C: Third Circle = No Control

When all the inhibitors and drivers have been assigned to one of the spheres, they will have a clear picture of their current situation. As the leader gathers up all the cards in the "C" outermost circle, the ones the group believes they have no control over, he or she throws them away in the wastebasket. The group can be instructed to not take any action on them since that would be a waste of time. Even talking and complaining about these drivers and inhibitors is a waste of time. Next, gather up all the cards in the "B" circle and put them in a file folder to be looked over later. Actually, you never really look at them again, but you can tell the group that if you want.

From this point on, only the drivers and inhibitors in the "A" circle will be addressed. By focusing on what they can control and not wasting their time, the group will be more effective.

This process is repeated for each of the top measures of success

WHAT CAN WE DO?

"A" Circle

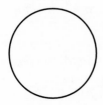

Brief your group to come to this meeting or meetings prepared to generate ways to weaken the inhibitors. By weakening them first, the drivers that are currently in place will begin to exert their influence. Without spending any extra time, money, or effort on the drivers, they will have a greater impact and begin to move the measure of success toward the ideal state.

At this meeting, record all the ideas to weaken the inhibitors on a flip chart. Don't stop at the first plausible idea or ideas, keep pushing the group, and encourage them to build off of each other's ideas. The goal at this stage is to generate a large quantity of ideas. Quality comes later; get them to brainstorm as large a list of possible actions as possible to weaken the inhibitors. Later, two or three months down the road, this process can be repeated with the focus on strengthening the drivers. At this time, with the inhibitors weakened or removed, the drivers will now have a bigger bang for the buck.

Record and distribute all the ideas generated in this meeting.

Repeat this process for each of the top measures of success

WHAT WILL WE DO?

H ere is where all this hard work pays off. Brief your group to come to this meeting or meetings prepared to discuss which of the ideas generated in the last stage will have the biggest and best impact to weaken the inhibitors.

The leader's job at this stage is to keep the group focused on their main measures of success. Any potential action should be clearly seen as having an impact on weakening the inhibitor. If the group struggles, you can always use another nominal group voting. Hopefully, the best actions, based on the main measures of success, become apparent to the group without that.

At the end of this meeting or meetings, the group should have some clear action steps to take. It is critical that those next action steps be assigned to individuals and that a timeline be established.

As before, repeat this process for each main measure of success. Also, remember to cycle back for each of those main measures in two or three months and run through this process to strengthen the drivers.

WHAT HAPPENED?

A t some regular intervals after the action steps have been implemented, take stock of what is happening. Gather the group and discuss what the main measures of success are telling you. Have your efforts produced positive results, negative, what?

If the measures of success have improved but that does not equate to success, maybe the main measures of success need to be reexamined. Goals and targets can move, regulations and customers' demands change. This process is not to be done just once, it can and should be an ongoing effort to identify and keep current on the main criteria for success. It should be expected that they will change and the group will continually need to adapt their efforts. Nothing, after all, stays the same.

Remember all those driver and inhibitor index cards from the "B" circle that you filed? When the group repeats the whole process from the beginning, they are likely to discover an interesting fact. Because they focused their efforts on what they really controlled, some of those items that they only influenced before have migrated into their sphere of control, the "A" circle. Or maybe their sphere of control has enlarged? Either way, by focusing on what you can do you demonstrate an ability to prioritize and get things done. That is a trait that leads to gaining more power and responsibility.

END

So why is this last section not written in the same story format as the rest of the book? Because the final story of this book is whether you can take the lessons and insights and make them work for you. That is a story that is yours to write. It is the story of "Plan your work and work your plan." It is not a new story; it is an old one. It is a story that can be repeated over and over again without getting old. This game plan has worked before to create better and more productive workplaces, and it can do the same for you in the future.

Write a good story! Send me an e-mail telling me your story at: tedb@tedbaumhauer.com.

I'd like to hear about it.

LITTLE BLUE PENGUIN
CHECKLIST

Checklist

❑ Group's ground rules

❑ Agreed main measures of success

❑ Starting point and target for each

❑ Drivers and inhibitors identified

❑ Possible action steps

❑ Best action steps identified

❑ Who, what, and when identified to assess progress and adjust if needed